MUSL M

This book is to be returned on or before the last date stamped below.

© 1988 Watts Books
Paperback edition 1995

This edition 1996

Watts Books
96 Leonard Street
London
EC2A 4RH

Franklin Watts Australia
14 Mars Road
Lane Cove
N.S.W. 2066

UK ISBN: 0 86313 673 7 (hardback)
UK ISBN: 0 7496 2270 9 (paperback)

Dewey Decimal Classification Number 297

Design: Edward Kinsey

Typesetting: Tradespools Ltd

Printed by G. Canale, Turin, Italy

The Publishers would like to thank
the Nazir family and all other
people shown in this book.

Sheikh Jamal M.A. Solaiman is
Imam of the Central Mosque,
Regents Park, London.

Note: Many of the photographs in
this book originally appeared in
'My Belief: I am a Muslim'

MUSLIM

Jenny Wood

Photographs: Chris Fairclough
Consultant: Sheikh Jamal M.A. Solaiman

Watts Books
London/New York/Sydney

These people are Muslims.
They follow a religion called Islam
which began in Arabia
over a thousand years ago.

Islam was begun
by the prophet Muhammad
who lived in the Arab city of Mecca.
Mecca is now the holy city of Islam.

Muslims believe that God's message,
as spoken to Muhammad,
is written in the Koran,
their Holy Book.
The Muslim name for God is Allah.

Muslims must wear clothes
that cover their bodies.
A man must cover his body
from the waist to the knees.

A Muslim woman must cover herself
from head to toe,
except for her hands and face.
Many Muslim women wear a long tunic
over loose trousers.

This is a mosque.
Muslims come here to worship Allah.
Mosques usually have a dome
and a tower called a minaret.

Before entering the mosque,
Muslims must take off their shoes.

Muslims have to make sure
they are clean before praying
to Allah. They wash their hands,
face, arms, head, ears,
and finally their feet.

When they pray, Muslims
must face Mecca, their holy city.
They sit on special prayer mats.
The prayers are led by an Imam.

15

Prayers last for about ten minutes. Women are not allowed to pray with the men. They worship in a different part of the mosque.

Every mosque has a Koran school, where Muslim children learn to read their Holy Book. Muslims must live according to the rules of the Koran.

The Koran is written
in Arabic script.
The pages are often
beautifully decorated.

Muslims read the Koran at home too.
They keep their copies of the Koran
wrapped in cloth, so that
they do not get dirty.

Muslims must pray to Allah
five times a day. At home,
as in the mosque, Muslims take off
their shoes and wash themselves.

Muslims have to obey special rules
about food. They are not allowed
to eat pork. All other meat
must be prepared in a special way,
known as "Halal".

Favourite meals are curries, kebabs and rice.

All Muslims wash and say prayers
before and after a meal.
The eldest person in the family
starts eating first.

A Muslim wedding is very colourful.
The bride dresses in red.
After the ceremony,
there is a wedding feast.

The bridegroom wears
a special head-dress.
He gives a gift of money
to his bride.

Muslims like to study the many books
on the teachings of Muhammad
and the rules of Islam.
They try to follow all the rules
and become good Muslims.

FACTS ABOUT MUSLIMS

Islam, the Muslim religion, is the second largest religion in the world. It has about 600 million followers.

In Britain, there are about one million Muslims. They come mainly from Pakistan, Bangladesh, India, and West and East Africa.

Muslims believe that the Koran contains the word of Allah, as told to the prophet Muhammad. Muhammad lived in the holy city of Mecca over a thousand years ago.

There are five things which all Muslims must do during their lifetime.
1. They must say that they believe there is no God but Allah.
2. They must say their prayers five times a day.
3. They must give money to the poor.
4. They must go without food or drink between dawn and dusk during the month of Ramadan, the ninth month in the Muslim year.
5. They must visit the holy city of Mecca.

GLOSSARY

Allah
The Muslim name for God.

Arabic
The language of the Arabs. The Koran is written in Arabic.

Halal
An Arabic word, meaning "allowed". It is used to describe food that has been prepared according to Muslim laws.

Imam
The person who leads the prayers in the mosque.

Islam
The Muslim religion.

Koran
The Muslim Holy Book.

Mecca
The Muslim holy city. It is in Saudi Arabia.

Mosque
The Muslim place of worship.

Muhammad
The founder of the religion of Islam.

Prophet
A religious teacher.

INDEX